# JESUS, WHO ARE YOU?

## JANNA ARNDT & KAY ARTHUR

**HARVEST HOUSE PUBLISHERS**
EUGENE, OREGON

All Scripture quotations are taken from the New American Standard Bible®, © 1960, 1962, 1963, 1968, 1971, 1972, 1973, 1975, 1977, 1995 by The Lockman Foundation. Used by permission. (www.Lockman.org)

Cover and interior illustrations by Tessa Sentell

Cover design by Connie Gabbert Design + Illustration

Back cover author photo by Nicole Higgins

Interior design by KUHN Design Group

HARVEST KIDS is a trademark of The Hawkins Children's LLC. Harvest House Publishers, Inc., is the exclusive licensee of the trademark HARVEST KIDS.

**Jesus, Who Are You?**
Copyright © 2020 by Precept Ministries International and Janna Arndt
Published by Harvest House Publishers
Eugene, Oregon 97408
www.harvesthousepublishers.com

ISBN 978-0-7369-7899-6 (pbk.)

**Printed in the United States of America**

20  21  22  23  24  25  26  27  28  / VP-SK /  10  9  8  7  6  5  4  3  2  1

For Oliver,
My precious grandson

The greatest gift I can give you is to show you
WHO Jesus is so you can choose to follow Him.
Jesus loves you so much, He gave His life for you!

I love you, Ollie,
Granna

*These things have been written so that you may believe that Jesus is the Christ, the Son of God; and that believing you may have life in His name.*

JOHN 20:31

# Contents

# An Important Note to Adults

## *(Please read this.)*

**Parents, grandparents, Sunday school teachers, and educators,**

Welcome to the Beginner Inductive Bible Study series—*inductive* Bible Studies that help young children learn how to read and study the Bible for themselves. This series also helps children develop important skills related to colors, shapes, positional concepts, reading, mathematics readiness, and dexterity as they learn God's Word.

Begin each day's study by reading the brief opening story aloud to the child. Put your finger under each word so the child will learn that words have meaning and are read from left to right. If the child has already learned how to read, let the child read the story aloud to you.

- When you come to the instructions, read them aloud to the child.

- When you see a verse of Scripture enclosed in a box, read the verse aloud one word at a time as the child repeats each word. Have the child touch each word while saying it out loud. This will teach the child to recognize words and to read from left to right.

- When you come to a question, ask the question out loud, and give the child time to think and then give an answer. Ask the 5 W's and an H questions: **WHO, WHAT, WHEN, WHERE, WHY,** and **HOW**. This will help kids uncover what the Bible says and develop their thinking and reasoning skills.

Activities like tracing a word, drawing or coloring a key word, coloring pictures, and so on will help children develop fine motor skills, which are essential for writing readiness. Make sure the child has a pencil for writing, crayons to color the pictures, and colored pencils for marking Scripture. Crayola erasable Twistables Colored Pencils have a built-in sharpener and eraser, which are great for young children.

When the child draws or colors a picture, ask them to tell you about what they have drawn or colored. Having them tell you from memory what they have learned develops their thinking, reasoning, and language skills.

As children follow directions, identify shapes and colors, and work with numbers, they develop their cognitive skills. As they answer questions and verbalize what they observe, they develop language skills.

Do not rush through this precious time with the child. Ask God to lead and guide you. Remember, you are giving this child incredible gifts: learning who Jesus is, learning how to read and understand God's Word, and spending time with you—one person God is using in their young life to love them, nurture them, and help them to grow and develop.

May God bless and use you!

*Janna and Ray*

*From childhood, you have known the sacred writings which are able to give you the wisdom that leads to salvation through faith which is in Christ Jesus.*

2 TIMOTHY 3:15

# COOPER, CALLIE, AND KATE

"Hi! My name is Cooper, and this is my sister, Callie. This is our dog, Kate. Callie and I love Kate.

"Kate can do funny things. She loves to sniff out clues and lick our faces. Watch out! Kate will lick your face too!

"Kate wants to help us learn about Jesus. Do you know **WHO** Jesus is?

"We do, and we want you to know Jesus too. We can find out **WHO** Jesus is by reading the Bible.

"The Bible is the most important book in the world. The Bible is God's words. The Bible is the truth."

"God uses the Bible to teach us. The Bible shows us **WHO** Jesus is, **WHAT** He does, and **HOW** we can know Him and do what is right."

# In the Beginning

*John 1:1-4*

The Bible is divided into two parts. The first part is called the Old Testament,

and the second part of the Bible is called the New Testament.

Before we read the Bible, we need to pray and ask God to teach us. Prayer is talking to God.

Let's pray and ask God to teach us as we read the Bible.

"God, thank You for giving me Your book, the Bible. I know the Bible is the truth. Please teach me how to read and understand the Bible so I can know truth for myself. Please teach me who Jesus is. Amen."

# DAY 1

# **WHEN** Was the Word?

"Cooper, come look at Kate," Callie called out. "Kate has her paws around the Bible! Kate wants to read the Bible too! Let's read the Bible to Kate to find out **WHO** Jesus is."

**WHO** is Jesus? Do you know? To find out the truth about Jesus, we need to read God's book, the Bible.

God had one of Jesus's disciples, John, write the Gospel of John in the Bible so we can learn **WHO** Jesus is.

The Gospel of John is in the second part of the Bible— the New Testament.

The word *gospel* means *good news*. The first four books in the New Testament are called Gospels because they tell the good news about Jesus. The Gospel of John is the fourth Gospel in the New Testament.

John is one of Jesus's disciples. Jesus's disciples are people who learn from Him and follow Him. That's why it is important to learn **WHO** Jesus is—so you can choose to follow Him too.

Let's look at the first verse in the Gospel of John to see **WHAT** John wants us to learn about Jesus.

Cooper and Callie want you to touch each word in John 1:1 as you say it out loud:

JOHN 1:1 "In the beginning was the Word, and the Word was with God, and the Word was God."

15

Turn back to page 15 and look at the words in John 1:1 that have an oval 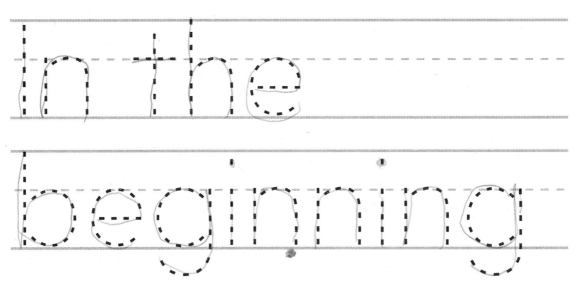 around them. These words tell us **WHEN** the Word was.

Trace the words below that tell us **WHEN** the Word was.

In the
beginning

All right! **WHEN** was the Word?

Touch each word you traced and say it out loud.

You did great! You just learned the Word was in the beginning. That means the Word has always been. Isn't that cool?

Cooper and Callie are so proud of you!

# WHO Was the Word With?

Look at Kate praying with Cooper and Callie!

Let's talk to God too!

"God, please teach me how to read and understand the Bible. I want to know **WHO** Jesus is. Thank You! Amen."

**WHAT** is the name of the Gospel we are studying to learn about Jesus? Do you remember? Say it out loud.

On the next page, trace the name of the Gospel we are studying.

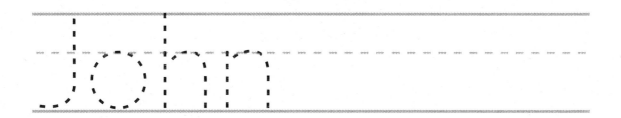

Now look at it. Touch it. Say it out loud.

Yesterday you learned something important about the Word in the Gospel of John. Do you remember what you learned?

Look at John 1:1 below. Let's say John 1:1 out loud. Touch each word as you say it.

JOHN 1:1 "In the beginning was the Word, and the Word was with God, and the Word was God."

**WHEN** was the Word? Say it out loud.

Take a green colored pencil and trace the oval around the words that tell you **WHEN** the Word was.

Look back at John 1:1. **WHO** was the Word with? Say it out loud.

Do you see the triangle over the word *God*? Use a purple colored pencil to trace the triangle. Color the inside of the purple triangle yellow.

When we study the Bible, we put a purple triangle over the word God and color it yellow. Doing this helps us see God in the Bible.

Trace the name of the person the Word was with.

You did it! You have learned two things about the Word. Can you say those two things out loud?

**WHEN** was the Word?

**WHO** was the Word with?

All right! Kate is so excited about what you have learned, she is wagging her tail! Way to go!

# WHO Is the Word?

"Stop, Kate!" Cooper shouted.

Kate ran around Cooper with her mouth full of colored pencils.

Callie laughed. "Kate thinks you're playing a game."

Cooper gave Kate a sign. "Sit, Kate!" Kate sat.

"Drop it!" Cooper said. Kate dropped the colored pencils.

"Good dog!" Cooper patted Kate's head. "Let's talk to God so we can learn more about the Word."

Did you talk to God today?

Look at John 1:1. Touch each word as you say it out loud.

JOHN 1:1 "In the beginning was the Word, and the Word was with God, and the Word was God."

**WHO** was the Word? Say it out loud.

Look at John 1:1 again. Use a purple colored pencil to trace the triangle over **WHO** the Word was.

Color the inside of the purple triangle yellow.

Trace the word that tells us **WHO** the Word was on the lines below.

The Word was...

Isn't that awesome! You learned something else about the Word. You now know three things about the Word. On the next page, trace the three things you have learned about the Word.

The Word was...

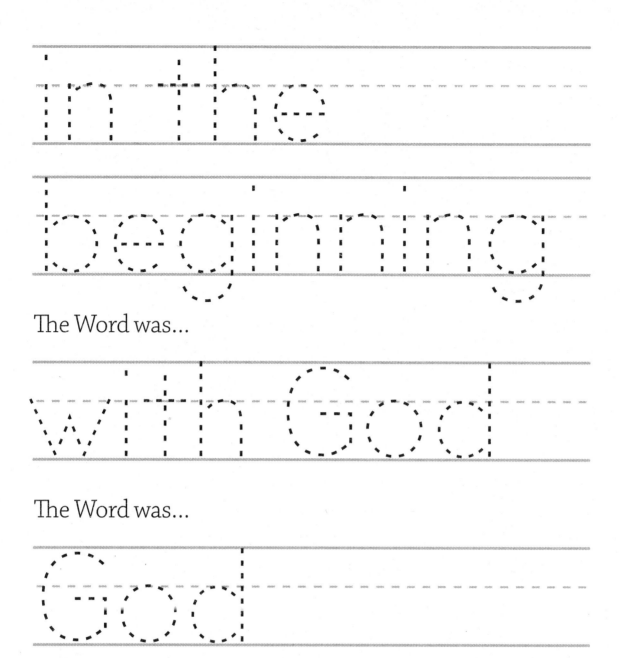

in the

beginning

The Word was...

with God

The Word was...

God

Great work! The Word and God were together in the beginning. The Word and God are both God. John shows us there are two people in the beginning who are God. You know one is God. **WHO** is the other person who is also God? **WHAT** is His name? Think about it.

Kate is running around barking again. She can't wait to find out!

# WHAT Did the Word Do?

"Hey, Callie, come look at Kate!" Cooper said. "Look at how still Kate is sitting."

"Oh, no, Cooper!" Callie cried out. "Snowball's in our yard. Grab Kate—quick, before she sees Snowball!"

It was too late! Kate spotted Snowball the cat. Cats make Kate crazy! Kate jumped up and pushed the screen out of the window.

"Oh, no!" Callie yelled. "Kate jumped out."

"Stay, Kate!" Cooper shouted out the window. Kate didn't stay. "Come back, Kate!" Kate ran as fast as she could. Kate chased Snowball the cat out of her yard!

"There she is!" Cooper shouted. "Kate chased Snowball to Mr. Tallent's yard. Look at her! She's jumping up and down on the fence. Kate is trying to get Snowball."

"Bad, bad dog!" Cooper pulled Kate down. "Go home, Kate!"

Kate panted as she trotted home. What an adventure! She almost caught Snowball the cat this time.

Now that Kate is home from her big adventure, Cooper and Callie are ready to talk to God to learn more about the Word.

Are you ready to pray? Talk to God and ask Him to teach you more about the Word in the Gospel of John.

"God, please teach me **WHO** the Word is and **WHAT** He does. Amen."

Let's read John 1:3 out loud. Touch each word as you say it.

> JOHN 1:3 "All things came into being through Him, and apart from Him nothing came into being."

Look at John 1:3. When John used the word *Him*, he was talking about the Word. **WHAT** do you see about the Word? Circle the correct answer below. Say it out loud.

**Nothing came into being through Him.**    **All things came into being through Him.**

WOW! All things came into being through the Word.

Look at the drawing on the next page. Connect the dots to discover **WHAT** John is showing you about the Word in John 1:3. Color the words.

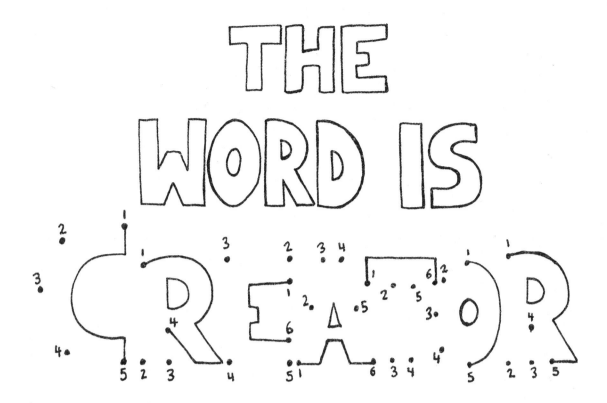

**WHO** is the Word? Say it out loud.

Amazing! You have discovered the Word is Creator! All things came into being through Him. The Word created the world with God.

In the beginning, there is someone **WHO** was with God and **WHO** is God, and He created the world with God.

Keep reading and studying the Bible to find out **WHO** this person is.

You learned something big today. Shout it out loud! The Word is Creator!

# WHAT Is in the Word?

"Hey, Cooper, let's go outside to learn about the Word today."

"That's a great idea, Callie! I'll get Kate. Let's hope Snowball stays in her yard today."

Talk to God and ask for His help as you study the Bible.

Let's read John 1:4 out loud. Touch each word on the next page as you say it.

JOHN 1:4 "In Him was [life], and the [life] was the Light of men."

Look at John 1:4. When John used the word *Him*, he was talking about the Word. **WHAT** was in Him? Say it out loud. Trace the answer on the line below.

In Him was...

Look back at John 1:4. Trace the rectangles around the word *life* with a green colored pencil and color the inside green. **HOW** many rectangles did you trace?

Look at John 1:4 again. **WHAT** was the life? Say it out loud. Circle the correct answer below.

**the Light of men**          **the darkness**

Look back at John 1:4. Color the word *Light* yellow.

AWESOME! You learned two new things about the

Word. You know there is life in the Word, and the life is the Light of men.

Let's review all you learned about the Word this week.

Draw lines from *The Word* to the words that tell you **WHAT** you discovered about the Word this week.

was in the beginning

was with God

was God

**The Word**        was in the beginning with God

all things came into being through Him (He created the world)

in Him was life

the life was the Light of men

Great work! Next week you will discover the Word's name. Kate is so excited! She wants to give you a good face-licking!

# WHO Is the Word?

*John 1:9-14; 8:12*

Last week you discovered some amazing things about the Word.

This week you are going to learn **WHO** the Word is. You are going to learn the Word's name! Isn't that exciting?

# The True Light

"Hey, Cooper, look at Kate!" Callie pointed outside.

"Kate is sniffing for clues," Cooper said.

"Oh, no!" Callie shouted. "Kate has spotted a bunny. Call her quick, Cooper!"

"Come, Kate!" Cooper called as he held up a biscuit.

Kate saw the biscuit and forgot all about the bunny.

"Whew, that was close!" Cooper exclaimed. Kate trotted to Cooper. "Good girl! It's time to talk to God." Kate laid down and bowed her head.

"God, thank You for giving us the Bible so we can know the truth. Please teach us **WHO** the Word is. Amen."

Look at John 1:9 below. Touch each word as you say it out loud.

JOHN 1:9 "There was the true Light which, coming <u>into the world</u>, enlightens every man."

Look at John 1:9. **WHAT** is the Light called? Say it out loud. Color the words *true Light* yellow.

Look back at John 1:9.

**WHERE** did the Light come? Say it out loud.

Trace the <u>double-underlined</u> words in green. They tell us **WHERE** the Light came.

Look at John 1:9 again. **WHAT** did the true Light do when it came into the world? Say it out loud. Trace the answer on the lines below.

The true Light...

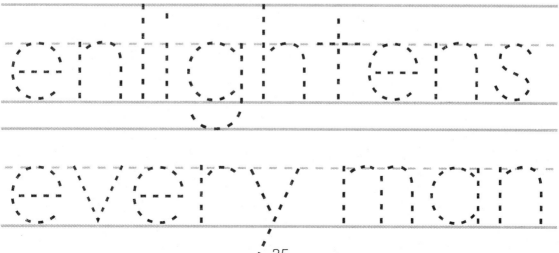

*Enlighten* means to give light, to give understanding to, to make to see.

Color the picture below that shows where the true Light came.

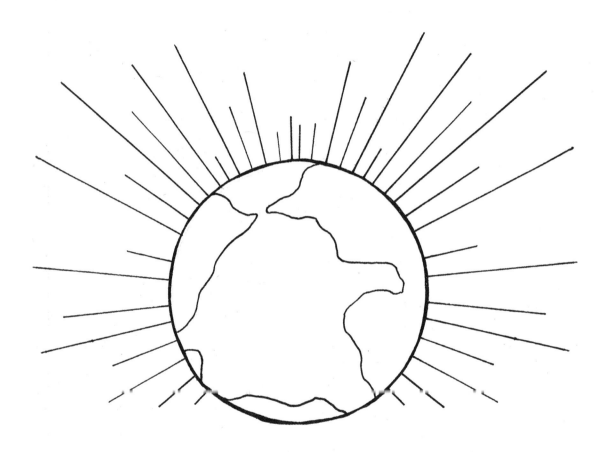

The Word is the true Light that came into the world to give understanding to every man. Isn't that awesome?

## DAY 2

# The World

Look at Kate. Kate is sniffing out more clues. Kate wants to learn more about the true Light that enlightens every man.

Talk to God and ask Him to help you understand what you learn about the true Light today.

Look at John 1:10 below. Touch each word as you say it out loud.

> JOHN 1:10 "He was in the world, and the world was made through Him, and the world did not know Him."

Look at John 1:10 again. The word *He* refers to the Light, who is also the Word. **WHERE** was He? Trace the answer on the lines on the next page.

37

He was in the...

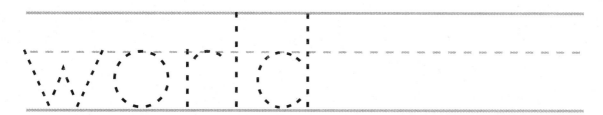

Touch the word and say it out loud.

Turn back to page 37 and look at John 1:10. Draw a blue oval (⬭) around the word *world* every place you see it.

Look at John 1:10 again. **HOW** was the world made? Trace the answer on the lines below.

The world was made...

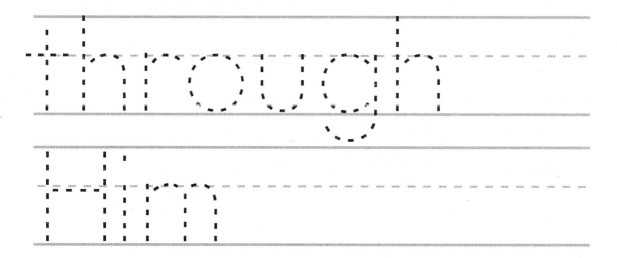

Touch each word and say it out loud.

Isn't that cool? Last week in John 1:3 you saw that the

Word made the world. Today in John 1:10 you see that the world was made through the Light, which is also the Word.

God has shown you two times that the Word—the Light—made the world.

Look at John 1:10 on page 37 again. Does the world know the true Light? Circle the correct answer below.

Yes                    No

The Word, the true Light, came into the world to give light and life to the world, but some people in the world will not know the true Light.

You are learning some very BIG and important things about the Word. **WHO** do you think the Word is?

**WHAT** is His name? We can't wait to find out what God says!

# WHO Become God's Children?

"Wow, Callie this is so cool!" Cooper said. The Word is the Light that came to give light and life to the world."

Callie looked at Cooper. "I wonder what we will learn about the Light today?"

"Let's talk to God so we can find out," Cooper said.

You pray too!

Let's read John 1:11. Touch each word on the next page as you say it out loud.

JOHN 1:11 "He came to His own, and those who were His own did not receive Him."

Look at John 1:11. The word *He* is talking about the Light, who is also the Word. **WHAT** do you see about Him?

Circle the correct answer below. Say it out loud.

**He came to strangers.**     **He came to His own.**

Look back at John 1:11 again. **WHAT** did His own people do? Trace the answer on the lines below.

They did not...

Let's look at John 1:12. Touch each word on the next page as you say it out loud.

41

JOHN 1:12 "But as many as received Him, to them He gave the right to become children of God, even to those who | believe | in His name."

Look at John 1:12. **WHAT** did He give the people who received Him? Trace the answer on the lines below.

He gave them the right to become...

Touch each word you traced and say it out loud.

Look back at John 1:12. **HOW** can people receive Him and become children of God?

Find the word that has a rectangle around it. Trace the rectangle with a purple colored pencil and color the inside green. **WHAT** do people have to do to receive Him? Say it out loud.

*Believe* means to put your trust in, to commit to, to accept what God says about someone or something.

Look at John 1:12 on page 42 again. **WHOSE** name do you need to believe in to become children of God? **WHO** is the *He* in this verse?

Circle the correct answers below.

     The Word      The true Light      John

If you believe—if you put your trust in the Word, the true Light—you will become God's child! That is so awesome! Tomorrow you will find out **WHO** the true Light is. HOW EXCITING! We can't wait! Neither can Kate—look how excited she is.

# WHO Is the Light?

"Wow!" Callie looked at Cooper. "We become children of God when we receive the true Light."

"That is so cool," Cooper said. "We know the Word is the Light, but...**WHO** is this person? **WHO** is the Light we need to receive to become children of God? This is something BIG we need to find out. Let's talk to God and ask for His help today."

You pray too!

You have learned some amazing things about the Light in John 1. Today, let's find out **WHO** the Light is.

Read John 8:12 on the next page. Touch each word as you say it out loud.

JOHN 8:12 "Then Jesus again spoke to them, saying, "I am the Light of the world; he who follows Me will not walk in the darkness, but will have the Light of life.""

**WHO** is speaking in John 8:12? Say it out loud. Trace the name on the lines below.

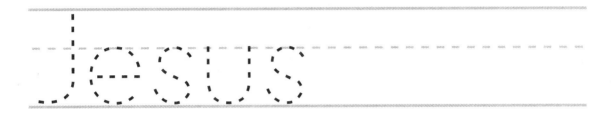

**WHO** did Jesus tell them He is? Say it out loud. Trace the answer on the lines below.

I am…

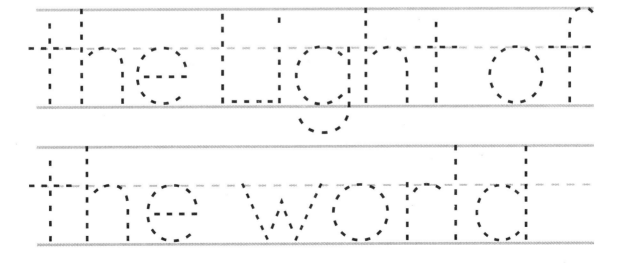

You did it! You have discovered **WHO** the Light is.

Say **WHO** the Light is out loud.

Look back at John 8:12 on page 45. Do you see a purple symbol over the word *Jesus* that looks like this? _____

When we study the Bible, we have a special way to mark the word *Jesus* and any words that are used to describe Him. First, we underline the word in purple. Then we draw part of a triangle on the right side. _____

Next we draw a line across the line on the right side to connect to the part triangle. _____

Then we color the inside yellow. Yellow is our color for God.

Look back at John 8:12 on page 45 and read it out loud again. Trace each symbol like this _____ with a purple colored pencil and color the inside yellow so you can see all the descriptions of Jesus in this verse.

Look back at John 8:12 on page 45 again. **WHAT** happens if you follow Jesus? Circle the correct answer below.

**You will walk in darkness.**                    **You will have the Light of life.**

Say it out loud.

**HOW** do you have the Light of life? Trace the answer on the lines below.

He who...

Say it out loud.

To follow Jesus means to do the things Jesus tells you to do, to be like Jesus.

Great work! You have just discovered that Jesus is the Light of the world. When you put your trust in Jesus and follow Him, you will have life! You become a child of God! Isn't that amazing?

Color the picture on the next page to show **WHO** Jesus is.

# JESUS IS THE LIGHT OF THE WORLD

# The Word Became Flesh

Cooper high-fived Callie. "We did it! We know **WHO** the Light of the world is. It's Jesus!"

"All right!" Callie shouted. "This is so AWESOME! We know the Light is the Word. And we know the Light is Jesus. So does that mean that Jesus is the Word?"

"There is only one way we can know for sure," Cooper said as Kate barked. "That's right, Kate. We need to see **WHAT** the Bible says. We can know **WHO** the Word is only by seeing **WHAT** God says. Let's ask God to show us."

"God, thank You for showing us that the Light of the world is Jesus. Show us **WHO** the Word is. Amen."

Look at John 1:14 below. Touch each word as you say it out loud.

JOHN 1:14 "And the Word became (flesh), and dwelt among us, and we saw His glory, glory as of the only begotten from the Father, full of grace and truth."

Look at John 1:14. **WHAT** did the Word become? Say it out loud.

Trace the oval ⬭ with a purple colored pencil.

When the Bible says the Word became flesh, it is telling us the Word became a human being like us.

Look back at John 1:14. **WHERE** did the Word dwell? Say it out loud.

Trace the double-underlined words with a green colored pencil. They tell **WHERE** the Word dwelt.

This means the Word—**WHO** is God, **WHO** was with

God in the beginning—left heaven, became a human being, and came to live among us on earth.

Look back at John 1:14 on page 50. **WHO** is the Word? Trace the answer.

The Word is the...

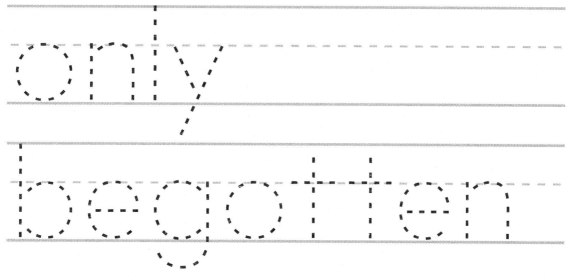

from the...

**WHO** is the Father? The Father is God.

Look back at John 1:14 on page 50. Draw a purple triangle △ over the word *Father* to show the Father is God. Color the inside of the purple triangle yellow.

**WHO** is God's only begotten Son? The phrase *only begotten* means the only one of His kind, the one and only.

**WHO** is God's only Son? **WHO** did God send from heaven to become a human being like us? Let's solve a puzzle to find out His name.

Look at the letters in the boxes below.

Find the box that has a 1 in it and write the letter in that box on the line with a 1 under it.

Put the letter from each box on the line that has the same number.

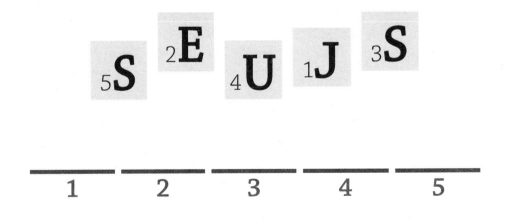

|  |  |  |  |  |
|---|---|---|---|---|
| 1 | 2 | 3 | 4 | 5 |

**WHO** is God's only begotten Son? Touch the name you just spelled and say it out loud.

Look back at John 1:14 on page 50. **WHAT** did they see about Jesus? Trace the answer on the lines below.

We saw...

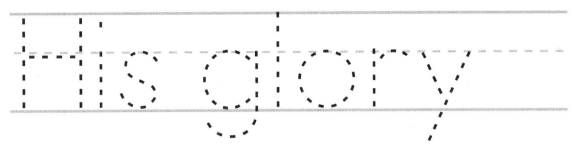

The Word, **WHO** is God, left heaven and became a man to live among man on the earth, and they saw His glory. AWESOME!

Color the picture on page 54 to show **WHO** the Word is.

Start by finding the places that have a black dot inside them and coloring them purple. Color the empty places that don't have a black dot yellow.

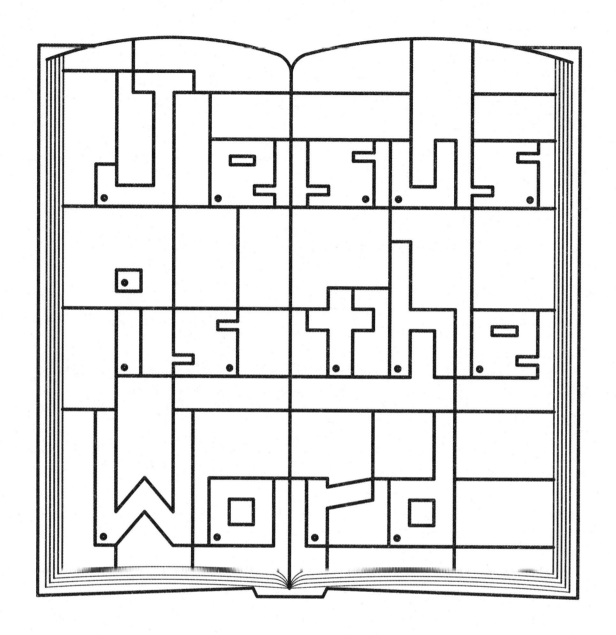

AWESOME! You did it! You know **WHO** the Word is. The Word is Jesus! Jesus is God. He was with God in the beginning. Jesus left heaven to become a man to live among us. Jesus is God's only begotten Son, full of grace and truth. That is so cool!

# The Savior

*John 1:1-49; 3:16-17*

Last week we discovered **WHO** the Word is. Say **WHO** the Word is out loud. The Word is Jesus!

We have learned some awesome things about **WHO** Jesus is in the Gospel of John.

**WHAT** will we learn today?

# Jesus Is…

"**WHY** is Kate barking so loud?" Callie asked Cooper.

"Look outside, Callie. Kate is telling us we are getting new neighbors."

"That's great!" Callie said. "I hope they have kids."

Kate barked and Cooper laughed. "Kate hopes they have a dog. Okay, Kate. It's time to review what we have learned about Jesus. Then we can go meet our new neighbors."

Callie laughed. "Let's hope they don't have a c-a-t."

Cooper agreed with Callie. "Come, Kate. Let's talk to God. Let's ask God to help us remember all the things we have learned about Jesus in John 1."

Let's do a crossword puzzle today to review all you have learned about Jesus.

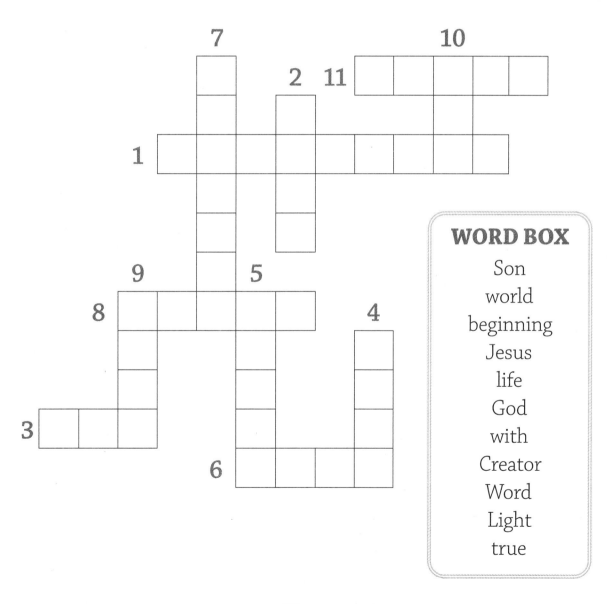

**WORD BOX**

Son
world
beginning
Jesus
life
God
with
Creator
Word
Light
true

Read John 1:1. Touch each word as you say it out loud.

> JOHN 1:1 "In the beginning was the Word, and the Word was with God, and the Word was God."

**WHEN** was the Word?

1. (across) John 1:1 "In the _____."

Say the answer out loud.

Look at the word box on page 57. Touch the correct answer.

Write the correct answer in the spaces beside the 1 in the puzzle.

Do the same thing for each question to solve the crossword puzzle.

**WHAT** did we see about the Word?

2. (down) John 1:1 "The Word was _____ God."

**WHO** was the Word?

3. (across) John 1:1 "The Word was _____."

Read John 1:4 below. Say it out loud.

> JOHN 1:4 "In Him was life, and the life was the Light of men."

**WHAT** was in Him?

4. (down) John 1:4 "In Him was _____."

**WHAT** was the life?

5. (down) John 1:4 "The life was the _____ of men."

Read John 1:9 below. Say it out loud.

> JOHN 1:9 "There was the true Light which, coming into the world, enlightens every man."

**WHAT** is the Light called?

6. (across) John 1:9 "The _____ Light."

Read John 1:10 on the next page. Say it out loud.

> **JOHN 1:10** "He was in the world, and the world was made through Him, and the world did not know Him."

**WHAT** does the world being made through Him show us about Him?

7. (down) He is the C __ __ __ __ __ r.

Read John 8:12 below. Say it out loud.

> **JOHN 8:12** "Then Jesus again spoke to them, saying, 'I am the Light of the world; he who follows Me will not walk in the darkness, but will have the Light of life.'"

**WHO** is Jesus?

8. (across) John 8:12 Jesus is the Light of the _____.

Read John 1:14 on the next page. Say it out loud.

JOHN 1:14 "And the Word became flesh, and dwelt among us, and we saw His glory, glory as of the only begotten from the Father, full of grace and truth."

**WHO** became flesh?

9. (down) John 1:14 "The _____ became flesh."

**WHO** is the Word?

10. (down) John 1:14 He is the only begotten from the Father. He is God's only begotten S __ n.

**WHO** is God's only begotten Son? **WHO** is the Word, God, the Life, the Light, and Creator?

11. (across) _____!

All right! Way to go! Are you wondering **WHY** John calls Jesus the Word? *Word* can mean *message*. The Bible is sometimes called God's Word because it is God's written message about Himself and about His Son, Jesus.

John calls Jesus the Word because Jesus served as

God's message about Himself to the world. God sent Jesus to show us the truth about **WHO** God and Jesus are. Isn't that amazing?

When Jesus spoke, He spoke God's words.

John shows us Jesus has always been with God.

Jesus was in the beginning. Jesus is God.

Jesus is Creator. Jesus is God's only begotten Son.

Jesus is life. Jesus is the Light of the world.

Jesus is God's message to us. Jesus speaks God's words! And when we believe in Jesus's name, we become children of God!

Incredible! Did you know all these wonderful things about Jesus? Look at all you have learned in God's Word! When you study God's Word, it makes Jesus and God happy. We are so proud of you!

# WHO Is the Lamb?

"Hey, Callie," Cooper called out. "Look! There's a girl with a white dog. Let's go meet our new neighbor."

Kate jumped up and barked.

"Kate wants to go too!" Callie said.

"Hi," Cooper called out. "I'm Cooper. This is my sister, Callie." Kate barked and wagged her tail. "And this is Kate, our wild pup."

"Hi. I'm Imani (ee-MAH-nee). This is my dog, Mozzie (MAH-zee)." Mozzie yowled.

"Did you hear that?" Callie asked. "Mozzie can talk!"

Imani laughed and Mozzie yowled again. "My dad is a Maasai (mah-SAI) pastor in Kenya. We are visiting while he speaks at mission conferences."

"That is so cool!" Cooper exclaimed. "Callie and I are studying the Bible to learn **WHO** Jesus is. Would you like to learn too?"

"That sounds like fun!" Imani replied. Kate got so excited she jumped up and licked Imani's face. Imani laughed. Kate licked Mozzie's face too.

Kate has made a new friend all the way from Kenya!

Let's talk to God.

Look at John 1:29. Can you touch each word as you say it out loud?

JOHN 1:29 "The next day he saw Jesus coming to him and said, 'Behold, the Lamb of God who takes away the sin of the world.'"

Look at John 1:29. The word *he* in this verse refers to John the Baptist. John the Baptist is not the same John who was Jesus's disciple and who wrote the Gospel of John. John the Baptist told others who Jesus is and how they could know and follow Him.

God tells us to do that too. That's why we are studying **WHO** Jesus is—so we can tell others the good news about Jesus and they can follow Him too!

Look at John 1:29 on page 64 again. **WHO** did John the Baptist see coming to him? Say it out loud.

Draw a purple cross symbol like this _____ ⚰ over **WHO** John the Baptist saw. Color the inside yellow.

Look back at John 1:29 on page 64. **WHAT** did John the Baptist call Jesus when he saw Him coming? Say it out loud. Trace the answer on the lines below.

Behold, the...

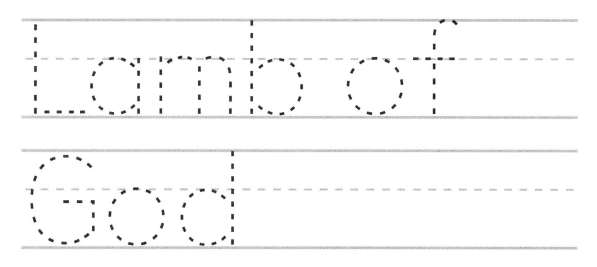

Way to go! You just learned another name that tells us **WHO** Jesus is.

**WHO** did John say Jesus is? Say it out loud.

Look back at John 1:29 on page 64. Draw a purple cross symbol like this _____✗ over the words that describe **WHO** Jesus is. Color the inside yellow.

Look at John 1:29 again. **WHAT** did John say the Lamb of God does? Say it out loud.

Color the word *sin* brown.

Look back at John 1:29 on page 64. **WHOSE** sin does the Lamb of God take away? Say it out loud.

Draw a blue oval ⬭ around this word.

**WHAT** is sin? In the Bible, God tells us that to sin is to know the right thing to do but not do it (James 4:17). To sin is to do what God says is wrong.

To sin is to do what we want to do instead of obeying God and doing things God's way.

God tells us sin separates us from Him.

But the good news is, God sent His Son Jesus, the Lamb of God, to take away the sin of the world. The Lamb of God came to save us.

**WHY** did God send Jesus to save us? Because He loves us so much!

Connect the dots and color the picture to show **WHO** came to save us.

Say it out loud: Jesus is the Lamb of God.

Kate and Mozzie are jumping up and down. They love your artwork!

# DAY 3

## WHAT Does Nathanael Know About Jesus?

"*Asante Sana*" (a-SAN-tay SAH-na), Imani said as she petted Kate. "*Asante sana* means *thank you very much* in Swahili. Thank you for inviting me to learn who Jesus is."

"How do you say 'You're welcome' in Swahili?" Callie asked as she petted Mozzie.

"*Karibu*" (ka-REE-boo), Imani replied.

Callie smiled at Imani. "*Karibu*."

"I wonder what we will learn today?" Cooper asked. "Let's talk to God."

Talk to God and thank Him for teaching you about Jesus.

Look at John 1:48 below. Can you touch each word as you say it out loud? Let's see what happens when Nathanael meets Jesus.

> JOHN 1:48 "Nathanael said to Him, 'How do You know me?' Jesus answered and said to him, 'Before Philip called you, when you were under the fig tree, I saw you.'"

Look at John 1:48. **WHO** is Nathanael talking to? Say it out loud.

Draw a purple symbol like this _____ over the person Nathanael is talking to and color it yellow.

Don't forget to draw this purple symbol and color it yellow over the pronouns (the other words for Jesus). Did you mark *Him* and *I*?

Look at John 1:49 below. Touch each word as you say it out loud.

> JOHN 1:49 "Nathanael answered Him, 'Rabbi, You are the Son of God; You are the King of Israel.'"

Look at John 1:49 on page 69. **WHAT** did Nathanael call Jesus? **WHO** did Nathanael say Jesus is?

Circle the correct answers below. Say them out loud.

**Rabbi**          **the Son of God**          **the King of Israel**

Look back at John 1:49 on page 69. Draw a purple symbol like this _____ over each description of Jesus in this verse and color them yellow.

Don't forget to mark the pronouns *Him* and *You* too!

You learned three new things about Jesus in John 1:49. Nathanael calls Jesus *Rabbi*, *the Son of God*, and *King of Israel*. How awesome!

*Rabbi* is the title the Jews used to greet and honor their teachers.

*Son of God* means God is the Father of Jesus.

*King of Israel* means someday Jesus is going to rule over His own people—the people of Israel, who are also called Jews. Nathanael knows Jesus is the promised Messiah, the Christ—the chosen and anointed One, who would save His people from their sins.

Nathanael knows Jesus is more than an ordinary man.

Look at the names Nathanael used for Jesus and the pictures below. Color each picture. Then draw a line from each name to match the picture that shows **WHO** Jesus is.

**Rabbi**

**Son of God**

**King of Israel**

Great work!

# WHO Does God Love?

"*Jambo* (JAHM-bo), Cooper. *Jambo*, Callie," Imani called out. "*Jambo* is the Swahili word for *hello*. Look, I brought a friend. This is Stephen. Stephen is visiting from Singapore."

"Hi, Stephen. I'm Cooper, and this is my sister, Callie." Kate jumped up and gave Stephen a good face-licking. "And that's Kate. Do you want to learn about Jesus too?"

"I sure do!" Stephen said.

"All right! Let's get our Bibles and talk to God."

Let's pray!

Now we are ready to read God's Word. Look at John 3:16. Can you touch each word as you say it out loud?

JOHN 3:16 "For God so loved the world, that He gave His only begotten Son, that whoever believes in Him shall not perish, but have eternal life."

Look at John 3:16. **WHO** loved the world? Say it out loud.

Draw a purple triangle △ over the word *God* and color the inside yellow. Don't forget to mark the other words for God too—the pronouns *He* and *His*.

Look at John 3:16 again. **WHO** did God give? **WHAT** is His name? Say it out loud.

Draw a purple cross symbol like this ____✗ over the words *only begotten Son* and color the inside yellow to show this is Jesus.

Look back at John 3:16. **WHY** did God give Jesus to the world? Say it out loud. Trace the heart ♡ with a red colored pencil and color the inside red.

Draw a blue oval ⬭ around the word *world*.

Look at John 3:16 on page 73 again. **HOW** do we receive eternal life? Say it out loud.

Circle the correct answer below. We receive eternal life by...

**doing good deeds**          **believing in Jesus**

Look at John 3:16 again on page 73. Draw a purple rectangle ⬜ around the word *believe* and color the inside green.

Look at John 3:16 again on page 73. **WHO** is the *Him* you are to believe in? Say it out loud.

Draw a purple cross symbol like this ✝ over the word *Him* and color the inside yellow to show this is Jesus.

To believe in Jesus means to put your trust in Him, to commit to Him, to accept what He says about someone or something.

**WHAT** will you receive if you believe in Jesus? Say it out loud.

Turn back to John 3:16 on page 73 and draw a green rectangle ☐ around these two words. Color the inside blue.

Isn't that wonderful? God loves the world so much, He gave us His Son Jesus so we can believe in Him and receive eternal life.

How AWESOME! Tomorrow we will discover **WHY** God sent His Son into the world. Kate and Mozzie can't wait to find out! They are barking and yowling in excitement!

# WHY Did Jesus Come?

"Hello!" Stephen called out from below the tree house.

"Hi, Stephen. Come on up!" Cooper called back. "Yesterday Imani taught us how to say *hello* in Swahili. What language do you speak in Singapore?"

Stephen smiled. "People in Singapore speak English and either Mandarin, Malay, or Tamil."

"Wow!" Callie said. "That's amazing! Can you speak one of those languages?"

"Yes," Stephen answered. "I can speak Malay."

"Cool," Cooper said. "Will you teach us how to say *hello* in Malay?"

"In the morning, you would say *Selamat pagi*" (SUH-lah-mat PAH-gee)."

Cooper tried it out: "*Selamat pagi*."

Stephen high-fived Cooper. "Great job!" Kate barked and Mozzie yowled.

Cooper said, "Yesterday we learned God loves the world

so much, He sent Jesus. I can't wait to see **WHY** Jesus came to the world!"

Don't forget to pray! Ask God to show you **WHO** Jesus is and **WHY** He came to the world.

Look at John 3:17. Can you touch each word as you say it out loud?

JOHN 3:17 "For God did not send the Son into the world to judge the world, but that the world might be saved through Him."

Look at John 3:17 on page 77. **WHO** sent His Son into the world? Say it out loud. Draw a purple triangle △ over the word *God* and color the inside yellow.

Look at John 3:17 on page 77 again. **WHO** is God's Son? **WHAT** is His name? Say it out loud.

Draw a purple cross symbol like this ___⁄ over the words *Son* and *Him* and color the inside yellow to show this is talking about Jesus.

**WHY** did God send His Son into the world? Say it out loud. Circle the correct answer below.

**to judge the world**          **to save the world**

Look back at John 3:17 on page 77. Draw a blue oval ⬭ around the word *world*.

Draw a red rectangle ▭ around the word *saved* and color the inside yellow.

Look back at John 3:17 on page 77. **WHAT** is the only way the world can be saved? Say it out loud. Trace the answer on the lines below.

Through…

Unbelievable! God loves us so much, He sent His Son Jesus to save us. You just learned something amazing about **WHO** Jesus is.

Trace the words below that tell us **WHO** Jesus is.

Jesus is…

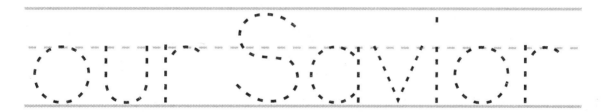

**WHY** would God send Jesus to save us? God tells us in Romans 3:23 we are all sinners. To sin is to do what we want to do instead of doing what God says is right. We sin when we disobey our parents, tell a lie, or are mean to our brothers and sisters. Sin is knowing the right thing to do but not doing it (James 4:17).

Because God is a holy God, He must punish sin.

But God loves us so much, He sent His Son Jesus Christ,

who never sinned, to die on the cross to pay for our sins and save us so we can live forever with Him.

God gives us a free gift that we cannot earn—salvation through His only begotten Son. Jesus Christ is our Savior!

To receive salvation, we have to believe that Jesus is God, that He died on the cross to pay for our sins, that He rose from the dead three days later, and that He is alive with God in heaven.

We have to agree with God that we are sinners and that we need Jesus to save us.

When we are ready to believe in Jesus—to put our trust in Him—we tell God we are sorry for our sins. We ask Him to forgive us for our sins. We ask Jesus to be our Savior. We repent (that means we turn away from doing things our way and do things God's way instead). We follow Jesus.

Then God forgives our sins, and we become children of God. God gives us the AWESOME gift of eternal life! **HOW** amazing is that? **WHO** is Jesus? Say it out loud. Fill in the blanks below.

Jesus is our S ___ ___ ___ ___ r!

Color the picture below to show **WHO** God and Jesus love.

Great artwork! Say thank You to God for His amazing love! Can you tell someone else **HOW** God sent Jesus into the world to save us?

# The Good Shepherd

*John 10*

Last week we met some new friends from other parts of the world. We discovered that God loved the world so much, He sent His Son Jesus to save the world. Nobody can save the world but Jesus! Isn't that incredible? Jesus is the only Savior!

# WHAT Does the Good Shepherd Do?

"I have a question," Stephen said. "Does 'God so loved the world' mean God loves everyone, no matter who they are or what they have done?"

"Yes, it does," Cooper said. "God loves all people. It doesn't matter what country we live in, the language we speak, whether we are a girl or a boy, the color of our hair or our skin, or whether we are good or bad. God loves everyone."

"That's why He sent Jesus," Callie said. "Jesus loves us so much, He left heaven to become a man and die on the cross to pay for all the wrong things anyone has ever done—or would do—so we can live forever with Him."

Imani clapped her hands. "*Yesu ni mwokozi* (YEH-soo nee mmwo-KO-zee)! Jesus is Savior!" Cooper, Callie, and Stephen high-fived Imani.

"Let's thank God for saving us."

All right! Say thank You to God for Jesus our Savior!

**WHAT** will we learn today?

Look at John 10:11 below. Can you touch each word as you say it out loud?

JOHN 10:11 "I am the good shepherd; the good shepherd lays down His life for the sheep."

**WHO** is speaking? Trace the answer on the lines below.

Look at John 10:11 on page 85. **WHO** does Jesus say He is? Say it out loud.

Draw a purple cross symbol like this ⟋ over the words that tell **WHO** Jesus is and color the inside yellow.

Can you count **HOW** many times you marked the words *good shepherd*?

Look at John 10:11 again on page 85. **WHAT** does the good shepherd do? Say it out loud.

Trace **WHAT** the good shepherd does on the lines below.

The good shepherd...

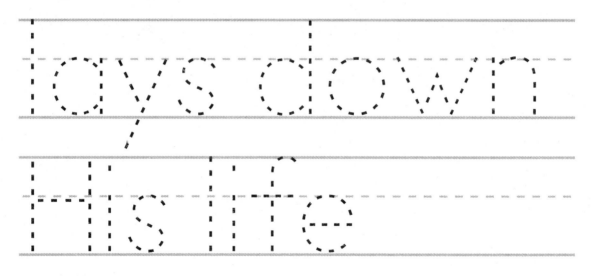

...for the sheep.

Great work! **WHO** is Jesus? Say it out loud.

You learned something new about Jesus. Jesus is the good shepherd who lays down His life for the sheep. **WHO** are the sheep? Mozzie and Kate can't wait to find out.

# The Hired Hand and the Wolf

"Look, Imani!" Callie called out. "Mozzie is herding Kate to us. Mozzie is trying to shepherd Kate."

"Silly puppy." Imani scratched Mozzie's ears. "Kate's not a sheep. Let's talk to God so we can learn more about the good shepherd."

Look at John 10:12. Touch each word as you say it out loud.

> JOHN 10:12 "He who is a hired hand, and not a shepherd, who is not the owner of the sheep, sees the wolf coming, and leaves the sheep and flees, and the wolf snatches them and scatters them."

Look at John 10:12. **WHO** sees the wolf coming? Say it out loud. Circle the correct answer below.

**the hired hand**       **the owner**       **the shepherd**

Look at John 10:12 again. **WHAT** does the hired hand do when he sees the wolf coming? Say it out loud.

Circle the correct answer below.

**protects and takes
care of the sheep**           **leaves the sheep
and flees**

Look back at John 10:12 on page 89. Draw a red
oval $\bigcirc$ around the words *the wolf.*

**WHAT** does the wolf do? Say it out loud.

Look at John 10:13 below. Touch each word as you say it
out loud.

> JOHN 10:13 "He flees because he is a hired hand
> and is not concerned about the sheep."

Look at John 10:13. **WHY** does the hired hand flee? Say
it out loud.

Underline the words that tell **WHY** the hired hand flees.

You did great! You learned the hired hand isn't the
shepherd, the owner of the sheep.

The hired hand is paid to take care of the sheep. He
doesn't care about the sheep. When trouble comes, the
hired hand flees and lets the wolf steal and scatter the
sheep.

**WHO** does John 10:11 teach us that Jesus is? Trace
**WHO** Jesus is on the lines on the next page.

Jesus is the...

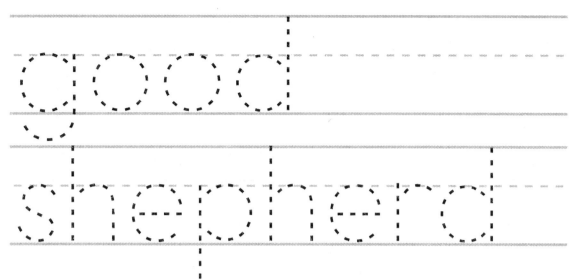

Touch each word and say it out loud.

Do you remember **WHAT** the good shepherd does? Say it out loud.

Jesus is the good shepherd. Jesus loves the sheep so much, He lays down His life for the sheep!

# WHO Are the Sheep?

"Look!" Cooper pointed to Kate and Mozzie. "Now Kate is trying to herd Mozzie."

Callie, Imani, and Stephen all laughed.

"Come, Kate! Come Mozzie!" Cooper called out. "Let's find out **WHO** the sheep are."

Don't forget to pray! Ask God to help you understand His Word.

We have learned Jesus is the good shepherd, but **WHO** are the sheep? Let's find out.

Today we are going to look at a verse in the book of

Isaiah. The book of Isaiah is in the first part of the Bible—the Old Testament.

Look at Isaiah 53:6 below. Touch each word as you say it out loud.

ISAIAH 53:6 "All of us like sheep have gone astray, each of us has turned to his own way; but the LORD has caused the iniquity of us all to fall on Him."

Look at Isaiah 53:6. **WHO** are like sheep? Say it out loud. Draw a blue cloud around those who are like sheep and give them feet and a head like this 🐑. Did you know God compares us to sheep?

Look at Isaiah 53:6 again. **HOW** are we like sheep? Say it out loud.

Trace the answer on the lines below.

Like sheep, we have...

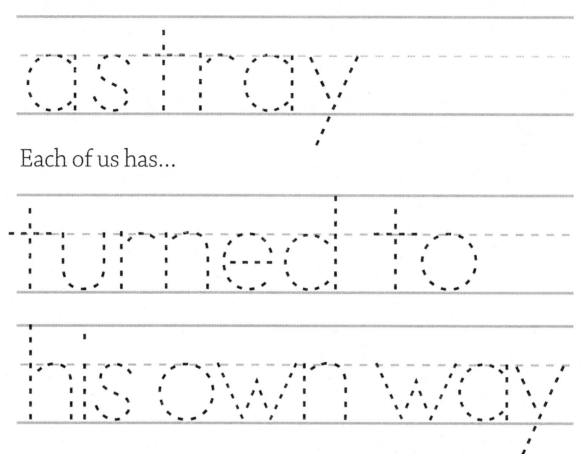

astray

Each of us has...

turned to

his own way

That means we stray from doing what God wants us to do. We turn to do what we want to do instead of what God says is right. We know what we are supposed to do, but we don't do it. Do you remember what that is called?

It's sin. To sin is to choose to do things our way instead of God's way! Have you ever gotten mad and stomped your feet or slammed a door because you were angry? Did you know it was the wrong thing to do, but you did it anyway?

That's sin!

Let's look at some fun facts about sheep to help you see

**WHY** God says we are like sheep and **HOW** Jesus is like the good shepherd.

Sheep are the dumbest of all animals. They are very stubborn. They want to go their own way. If they are left on their own, they will go the wrong way, eat the wrong food, drink the wrong water, and even wander right off a cliff.

Sheep need a shepherd to guide them to keep them from doing the wrong thing and getting into trouble. The shepherd provides the right food and water and keeps the sheep out of trouble.

Sheep get scared very easily. Sometimes they get so confused, they run right into danger instead of running away from it. The shepherd calms the sheep so they don't panic. The shepherd keeps the sheep safe.

Sheep are helpless and defenseless. They don't call out or run when they are in danger. They freeze. Sheep need the shepherd to watch out for them. The shepherd protects the sheep from wild animals. He drives away the animals who try to harm the sheep.

The shepherd lays down in the door of the sheepfold where the sheep sleep to protect the sheep from thieves and animals who would steal or harm the sheep. The shepherd lays down his life to protect the sheep.

Sheep do what other sheep do. If one sheep gets scared and runs, they all run. They follow other sheep.

Sheep need a shepherd to lead and guide them—to keep them going the right way so they don't get into trouble following other sheep. Have you ever done something your friends wanted you to do even though you knew it wasn't okay? Maybe you did it anyway so you would fit in. That's like sheep following each other right into trouble.

**WHO** is the good shepherd? Say it out loud.

**WHO** are the sheep? Say it out loud.

Look back at Isaiah 53:6 on page 93. **WHAT** did God cause to fall on Him (Jesus)? Say it out loud.

Circle the correct answer below. God caused...

**our goodness to
fall on Him**            **our iniquity (our sin)
to fall on Him**

Jesus was perfect. He never sinned. God loves us so much, He took all our sins and put them on Jesus.

Jesus died on the cross to pay for our sins.

**WHO** is Jesus? Say it out loud. Trace the answer on the lines on the next page.

Jesus is the...

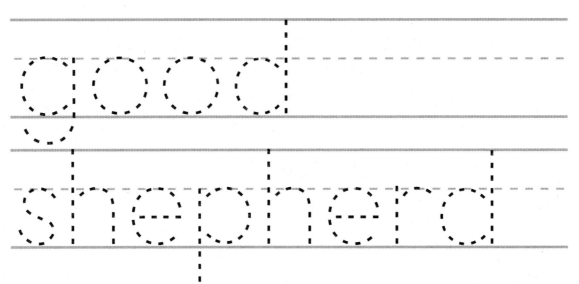

Jesus leads and guides us. He protects us from harm. He keeps us safe. Jesus laid down His life for us, His stubborn sheep. Isn't Jesus wonderful?

# DAY 4

# WHO Knows the Shepherd?

"Good catch, Kate!" Cooper said as Kate jumped in the air to catch the frisbee. "Here comes Callie with Stephen, Imani, and Mozzie. It's time to learn more about Jesus, the good shepherd." Kate barked in agreement and ran to see Mozzie.

Talk to God!

Look at John 10:14 below. Touch each word as you say it out loud.

JOHN 10:14 "I am the good shepherd, and I know My own and My own know Me."

Look at John 10:14. **WHO** is Jesus? Say it out loud.

Draw a purple cross symbol like this _____ over the words that show **WHO** Jesus is and color the inside yellow. Don't forget to mark the other words that refer to Jesus—the pronouns *I*, *My*, and *Me*—the same way.

Look at John 10:14 again. **WHO** does the good shepherd know? Say it out loud.

Draw a blue cloud around **WHO** the shepherd knows and give it feet and a head like this .

Look back at John 10:14. **WHO** does the shepherd's own know? Say it out loud.

**WHO** does the word *Me* refer to? Trace the answer on the line below.

Jesus, the good shepherd, knows the sheep that belong to Him. The sheep that belong to the good shepherd believe in Him. They are children of God! Jesus knows every sheep that is His! He knows them by name—how amazing is that?

# WHO Hears the Shepherd's Voice?

"Come, Kate!" Cooper called out. "It's starting to rain. Come inside!" Kate raised her head to look at Cooper.

Kate didn't move. Callie laughed. "Kate is pretending to be a stubborn sheep."

Cooper called again. "Come, Kate. Come get a biscuit." Kate jumped up and ran inside.

Let's learn more about our good shepherd. Don't forget to pray!

Look at John 10:27. Touch each word as you say it out loud.

> JOHN 10:27 "My sheep hear My voice, and I know them, and they follow Me."

Look at John 10:27. **WHOSE** voice do the sheep hear? Say it out loud.

Draw a purple cross symbol like this _____ ⅄ over the words *My*, *I*, and *Me* and color the inside yellow.

Look at John 10:27 again. **WHAT** do Jesus's sheep do? Say it out loud. Circle the correct answer below.

**follow Jesus**          **do what they want to do**

All right! If we belong to Jesus, we will hear the good shepherd's voice and follow Him.

So, **WHAT** does it mean to follow Jesus? It means...

You know **WHO** Jesus is. He is the Son of God.

You have believed in Him and asked Him to be your Savior.

You talk and listen to God. That's called prayer.

You obey.

You do the things that please God and Jesus.

You love other people.

You are kind.

You help others.

You praise God and thank Him.

You share.

You tell other people about Jesus.

Do you do these things? Go back and circle the things you do to show you love Jesus and want to be like Him.

Now, doing these things doesn't save us and make us Jesus's sheep. We are saved by trusting Jesus, by believing in Him. We do these things because we love Jesus and want to please Him by obeying Him. We want to be like Jesus.

Look at the picture of the good shepherd and the sheep

below. Color the sheep that have words written in them that show you follow the good shepherd—Jesus.

**FINISH**

OBEY GOD

BE KIND

TELL A LIE

TALK BACK TO PARENTS

LOVE OTHERS

TELL PEOPLE ABOUT JESUS

BE MEAN

DON'T SHARE

PRAY

**START**

You did it! You followed the good shepherd!

# The Resurrection and the Life

*John 11*

Last week you learned how to follow Jesus. Jesus is the good shepherd, who lays down His life for the sheep.

This week you are going to discover something incredible about Jesus. We can't wait!

## Jesus's Friend Lazarus

"*Jambo*, Imani," Cooper called out from the treehouse. "*Selamat pagi*, Stephen! Come on up. Kate can't wait to see Mozzie!"

Mozzie ran up the slide to get inside the treehouse.

Imani laughed. "Mozzie is going to miss Kate when we go home next week."

"We're going to miss all of you," Callie said as she patted Mozzie's head. Kate barked. "Kate is going to miss Mozzie too!"

"Sit, Kate! Sit, Mozzie! It's time to talk to God," Cooper said. Kate and Mozzie lay down and bowed their heads.

Don't forget to talk to God.

Today we are going to learn about Lazarus and his sisters, Mary and Martha. Lazarus, Martha, and Mary were Jesus's friends. Jesus loved them. Lazarus's sisters sent Jesus a message to tell Him Lazarus was sick. But instead of hurrying to Lazarus's house, Jesus waited two more days. **WHY** would Jesus do that? Let's find out.

Look at John 11:14 below. In this verse, Jesus is talking to His disciples about Lazarus. Touch each word as you read it out loud.

JOHN 11:14 "So Jesus said to them plainly, 'Lazarus is dead.'"

Look at John 11:14. **WHAT** does Jesus tell His disciples about Lazarus? Say it out loud.

Circle the correct answer below.

**Lazarus is sick.**          **Lazarus is dead.**

Look at John 11:15. Touch each word as you read it out loud.

> JOHN 11:15 "And I am glad for your sakes that I was not there, so that you may believe; but let us go to him."

Look at John 11:15. **WHY** was Jesus glad He wasn't there when Lazarus got sick? Say it out loud. Trace the answer on the lines below.

So that you may...

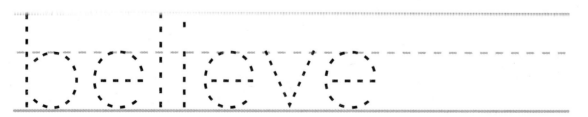

Look back at John 11:15. Draw a purple rectangle around the word *believe* and color the inside green.

Look at John 11:17 below. Touch each word as you say it out loud.

JOHN 11:17 "So when Jesus came, He found that he had already been in the tomb four days."

Look at John 11:17. **HOW** many days had Lazarus been in the tomb? Say it out loud.

Draw a green oval ⬭ around the number of days Lazarus had been in the tomb.

Wow! You have discovered Jesus's friend Lazarus has died. He has been in the tomb for four days! You also saw Jesus tell His disciples He was glad He wasn't there. **WHY** was Jesus glad? **WHAT** did He want the disciples to do? Say it out loud.

Do you know **WHAT** Jesus wanted His disciples to believe? Think about it.

Tomorrow we will learn more. Great job!

# WHO Do You Ask?

"Look, Callie!" Cooper called out. "Kate and Mozzie are playing tug-of-war."

Kate tugged hard on her end of the rope. Mozzie pulled back. Kate pulled with all her might and yanked Mozzie across the yard.

"Let go of the rope, Mozzie!" Cooper ran to Mozzie. "Are you all right?"

Mozzie popped up and licked Cooper on the nose. "Okay, you two, game time is over." Cooper scratched Mozzie's ears. "It's time to read God's Word."

Talk to God so you can read His Word.

Yesterday we learned that Jesus's friend Lazarus got sick and died. Today we are going to find out what happens when Jesus arrives and sees Martha.

Look at John 11:21 below. Touch each word as you read it out loud.

JOHN 11:21 "Martha then said to Jesus, 'Lord, if You had been here, my brother would not have died.'"

Look at John 11:21. **WHAT** did Martha say to Jesus? Say it out loud. Circle the correct answer below.

**If You had been here, my brother would not have died.**

**Why did You let my brother die?**

**WHAT** else does Martha say? Look at John 11:22 below. Touch each word as you say it out loud.

> JOHN 11:22 "Even now I know that whatever You ask of God, God will give You."

Look at John 11:22. **WHAT** does Martha say Jesus can do? Say it out loud. Trace the answer on the line below.

ask God

Look back at John 11:22. Draw a purple oval 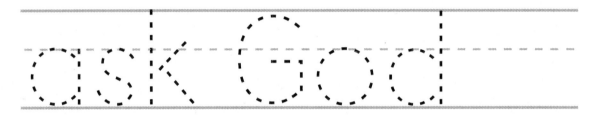 around the word *ask* and color the inside pink.

Draw a purple triangle △ over **WHO** Jesus can ask and color the inside yellow.

Look at John 11:22 again. **WHAT** will God do when Jesus asks? Say it out loud.

Trace the answer on the lines below.

God will...

give You

whatever...

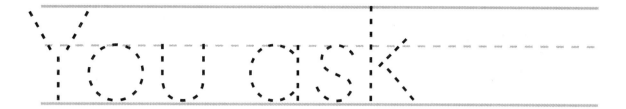

**HOW** can you ask God to help you? Let's solve a puzzle to find out.

Look at the letters in the boxes below.

Find the box that has a 1 in it and write the letter in that box on the line with a 1 under it.

Put the letter from each box on the line that has the same number.

**HOW** can you ask God?

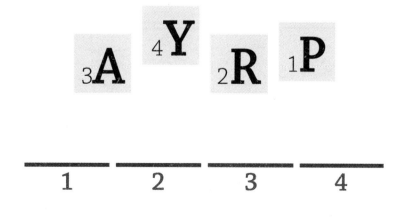

Prayer is talking to God. We can pray and ask God anything. Martha knows God will hear Jesus and give Jesus whatever He asks.

Tomorrow we will find out **WHAT** Martha knows about Jesus. We can't wait!

# Do You Believe?

"Isn't it great?" Imani said. "We can go to God and ask Him to help us, just like Jesus did."

"It's pretty amazing!" Cooper agreed. "Let's ask God for His help today."

Did you ask God to help you?

Look at John 11:23-24 on the next page. Touch each word as you read these two verses out loud.

JOHN 11:23 "Jesus said to her, 'Your brother will rise again.'"

JOHN 11:24 "Martha said to Him, 'I know that he will rise again in the resurrection on the last day.'"

Look at John 11:23. **WHAT** does Jesus tell Martha about her brother, Lazarus? Say it out loud. Circle the correct answer below.

**I am sorry your brother died.**

**Your brother will rise again.**

Lazarus is dead. He has been dead four days. Jesus says Lazarus isn't going to stay dead, but will rise again (be made alive). That is pretty amazing!

Look at John 11:25 below. Touch each word as you say it out loud.

JOHN 11:25 "Jesus said to her, 'I am the resurrection and the life; he who believes in Me will live even if he dies.'"

Look back at John 11:25 on page 118. **WHAT** does Jesus tell Martha about Himself? Say it out loud. Trace the answer on the lines below.

I am the...

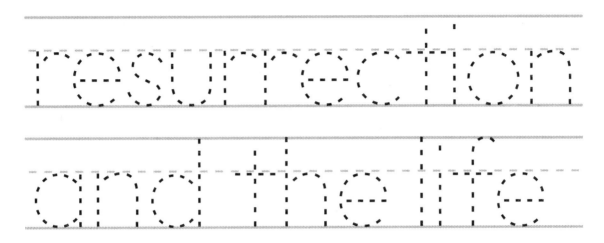

Look back at John 11:25 on page 118 again. Draw a purple cross symbol like this ⟍ over the words that tell us **WHO** Jesus is. Color the inside yellow.

Don't forget to mark the words *Jesus* and *Me* too!

To be resurrected means to be raised from the dead.

Jesus is telling Martha He is the resurrection and the life. That means Jesus has power over death! He can make those who have died alive again. WOW!

Look at John 11:25 on page 118 again. **HOW** are you going to live, even if you die? **WHAT** do you have to do? Say it out loud.

Draw a purple rectangle 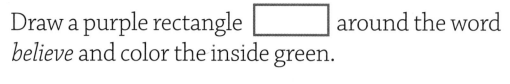 around the word *believe* and color the inside green.

Look back at John 11:25 on page 118. **WHO** do you need to believe in? Say it out loud. Trace the answer on the line below.

Look at John 11:26 below. Touch each word as you say it out loud.

> JOHN 11:26 "And everyone who lives and believes in Me will never die. Do you believe this?"

Look at John 11:26. **WHAT** happens to anyone who believes in Jesus? Say it out loud.

Circle the correct answer below.

**They will die.**　　　　　**They will never die.**

WOW! How amazing is that? If you believe in Jesus, you will never die! Because sin and death entered the world, our bodies will die (unless we are alive when Jesus comes back again). But if we believe in Jesus, if we put our trust in Him, He will raise us from death and give us eternal life in brand-new bodies.

When Jesus died on the cross, He paid for all our sins, so sin and death no longer have power over us. When Jesus was raised from the dead three days later, He conquered death. If we belong to Jesus, we will be raised too! That's why Jesus says everyone who believes in Him will never die. Those who believe in Jesus won't be dead forever—they will come to life again and be given new bodies.

**WHO** is Jesus? Shout it out loud—Jesus is the resurrection and the life! Isn't that incredible!

# Jesus Is the Christ

"How awesome!" Stephen said. "If we believe in Jesus, we will be raised from the dead and have eternal life!"

Imani smiled and clapped her hands. "*Asante Mungu*" (a-SAN-tay MOON-goo)—thank You, God!"

"**WHO** is Jesus?" Cooper asked. "Let's say it together. Jesus is the resurrection and the life!" Kate and Mozzie got excited and tried to lick all their faces.

Why don't you thank God for all you have learned?

Look at John 11:26-27. Touch each word as you read these verses out loud.

> JOHN 11:26 "Everyone who lives and believes in Me will never die. Do you believe this?"
>
> JOHN 11:27 "She said to Him, 'Yes, Lord; I have believed that You are the Christ, the Son of God, even He who comes into the world.'"

Look at John 11:26-27. Every time you see the word *believe*, draw a purple rectangle [    ] around it and color the inside green.

Jesus asks Martha if she believes.

Look at John 11:27 again. **HOW** does Martha answer Jesus? Say it out loud. Circle the correct answer below.

**No, I don't believe.**          **Yes, Lord, I have believed.**

Look back at John 11:27. **WHAT** does Martha believe? **WHO** is Jesus? Trace the answer on the lines on the next page.

Jesus is the...

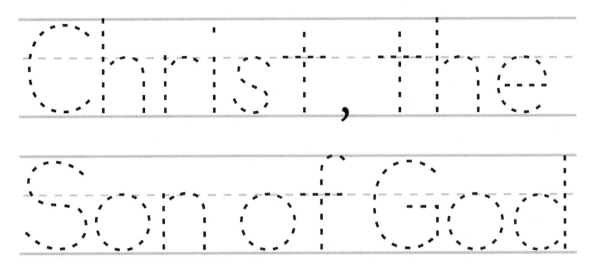

Touch each word you traced and say it out loud.

Look back at John 11:27 on page 123. Draw a purple cross symbol like this _____ over the words that tell us **WHO** Jesus is. Color the inside yellow.

Martha believed! She knows **WHO** Jesus is. Martha calls Jesus *Lord*! This title is given to God and means *Master* and *Owner*. To call Jesus *Lord* is to bow to Jesus as God and to give Him ownership by letting Him take over and rule your life.

Martha calls Jesus the Christ. She knows Jesus is the promised Messiah who would come to save His people from their sins.

And Martha knows Jesus is God's only begotten Son.

Can you find the words that describe Jesus in the puzzle below? The answers go across → and down ↓ in the puzzle. Look for the titles *Lord*, *Christ*, *Son of God*, and *Messiah*.

| C | M | E | S | S | I | A | H |
|---|---|---|---|---|---|---|---|
| H | T | R | W | F | G | H | L |
| R | J | L | Y | S | V | B | O |
| I | D | A | S | Q | W | U | R |
| S | O | N | O | F | G | O | D |
| T | L | D | P | S | K | L | R |

Martha believed in Jesus. Do you?

Tomorrow we will find out **WHAT** happens when Jesus goes to Lazarus's tomb. Kate and Mozzie are running around like crazy pups! They can't wait to find out!

# Jesus's Awesome Power

"All right!" Cooper exclaimed. "Martha believed! I can't wait to see what happens at the tomb."

"Me too!" Stephen said. "But I'm a little sad too. Today is our last day to learn about Jesus with you. Tomorrow Imani and Mozzie go home to Kenya, and I go home to Singapore."

Imani smiled. "But we can be happy because we can show kids in our countries how to discover **WHO** Jesus is too!"

"That's right!" Callie agreed. "You can share Jesus with kids in your neighborhood. That's pretty cool too!"

Talk to God. Ask Him to show you someone you can tell about Jesus too!

Look at John 11:38 below. Touch each word as you say it out loud.

> JOHN 11:38 "So Jesus, again being deeply moved within, came to the tomb. Now it was a cave, and a stone was lying against it."

Look at John 11:38. **WHERE** did Jesus go? Say it out loud.

Double-underline the words in green to show **WHERE** Jesus went.

Look at John 11:39 below. Touch each word as you say it out loud.

> JOHN 11:39 "Jesus said, 'Remove the stone.' Martha, the sister of the deceased, said to Him, 'Lord, by this time there will be a stench, for He has been dead four days.'"

Look at John 11:39 on page 127. **WHAT** did Jesus tell them to do? Say it out loud.

Trace the rectangle ☐ with a blue colored pencil to show what Jesus told them to do.

**WHAT** did Martha say? Hold your nose and say it out loud.

**HOW** long has Lazarus been dead? Say it out loud.

Look back at John 11:39 on page 127. Draw a green oval ⬭ around **HOW** long Lazarus has been dead.

Look at John 11:41 below. Touch each word as you say it out loud.

JOHN 11:41 "So they removed the stone. Then Jesus raised His eyes, and said, 'Father, I thank You that You have heard Me.'"

Look at John 11:41. **WHAT** does Jesus do? Say it out loud.

**WHAT** is this called? Do you know? Jesus is talking to the Father. Jesus is praying.

Look back at John 11:41. **WHAT** did Jesus say to the Father? Trace the answer below.

Father, I...

thank You
that You
have
heard Me

Jesus thanks God for what God is going to do through Him. Jesus is giving God the glory. Everything Jesus did was to point people to God. Remember, Jesus is God's message to the world.

**WHAT** happens after Jesus prays? Look at John 11:43 on the next page. Touch each word as you say it out loud.

JOHN 11:43 "When He had said these things, He cried out with a loud voice, 'Lazarus, come forth.'"

Look at John 11:43. **WHAT** did Jesus cry out?

Say it out loud.

Draw a blue rectangle [ ] around **WHAT** Jesus said.

Look at John 11:44 below. Touch each word as you say it out loud.

JOHN 11:44 "The man who had died came forth, bound hand and foot with wrappings, and his face was wrapped around with a cloth. Jesus said to them, 'Unbind him and let him go.'"

Look at John 11:44 again. **WHAT** happened to Lazarus? Say it out loud. Trace the answer on the lines below.

The man who died...

came

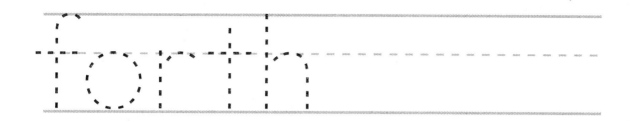

Look at Jesus's AWESOME POWER! Lazarus, who was dead, came forth. Jesus raised Lazarus from the dead! Lazarus is alive!

Now we know **WHY** Jesus was glad He wasn't there when Lazarus got sick and died. He wanted people to see **WHO** He is and His amazing power over death so they could believe in Him.

**WHAT** happened after Jesus raised Lazarus? Did people believe in Jesus after seeing His awesome power? Look at John 11:45 below.

JOHN 11:45 "Therefore many of the Jews who came to Mary, and saw what He had done, believed in Him."

Look at John 11:45. Draw a purple rectangle around the word *believed* and color the inside green.

Did people believe? Say it out loud!

Yes—they did! Color the picture below to show just **HOW** amazing and powerful Jesus is.

# JESUS IS THE RESURRECTION AND THE LIFE

Beautiful artwork! Say it out loud one more time—
**WHO** is Jesus? Jesus is the resurrection and the life!

# The Way, and the Truth, and the Life

*John 14:1-6; 16:33; 20:31*

Isn't Jesus powerful? Jesus raised Lazarus from the dead! **WHO** is Jesus? Say it out loud.

Jesus is the resurrection and the life! Amazing!

**WHAT** will we learn this week?

# Don't Be Troubled

Callie sighed. "I miss Stephen, Imani, and Mozzie. It was so much fun learning about Jesus with them."

"It sure was." Cooper agreed. "Kate looks sad too!"

"I know what will cheer us up. Let's continue our adventure with Jesus. Let's talk to God."

You talk to God too! Ask God to help you.

Look at John 14:1 below. Touch each word as you say it out loud.

> JOHN 14:1 "Do not let your heart be troubled; believe in God, believe also in Me."

Look at John 14:1 on page 134. Jesus is speaking to His disciples. **WHAT** is the first thing Jesus said to them? Say it out loud. Trace the answer on the lines below.

Do not let your...

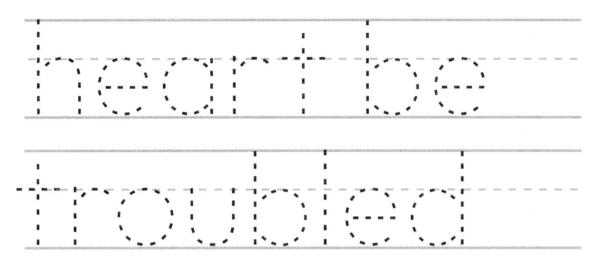

Look back at John 14:1 on page 134. Trace the heart ♡ with a red colored pencil and color the inside red.

Draw a black oval ⬭ around the word that tells the disciples what their hearts shouldn't be.

**WHY** are the disciple's hearts troubled? Jesus has just told His disciples He will be going away and leaving them.

The time is coming for Jesus to die on the cross to pay for our sins. The disciples are confused and discouraged. They don't understand why Jesus must leave them.

Look back at John 14:1 on page 134. **WHAT** does

Jesus say after He tells them not to let their hearts be troubled? Say it out loud.

Draw a purple rectangle [ ] around the word *believe* every time you see it and color the inside green.

Look at John 14:1 again on page 134. **WHO** are they to believe in? Say the names out loud.

Do you remember how to mark words that refer to God and Jesus? Look back at John 14:1 and mark the words *God* and *Me*.

Jesus is telling the disciples not to be upset or worried, but to trust God and to trust Him.

Look at John 14:2 below. Touch each word as you say it out loud.

JOHN 14:2 "In My Father's house are many dwelling places; if it were not so, I would have told you; for I go to prepare a place for you."

Look at John 14:2. **WHERE** is Jesus going? Say it out loud.

Trace in green the double-underlined words that tell **WHERE** Jesus is going.

**WHO** is Jesus's Father? Say it out loud.

Do you know **WHERE** God's house is? Trace the answer on the lines below. Say it out loud.

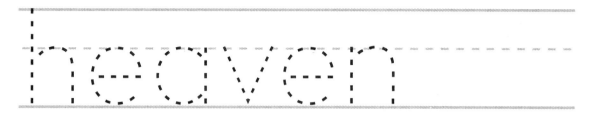

Look back at John 14:2 on page 136. **WHY** is Jesus going to His Father's house? Say it out loud. Circle the correct answer below.

**Jesus is tired of living on earth.**

**Jesus is going to heaven to prepare a home for us.**

All right! How cool is that? Jesus is going to heaven to prepare a place for us to live! Isn't that wonderful? Look at how much Jesus loves us!

# HOW Will We Get There?

"Come, Kate!" Cooper called out. "We are going on a BIG adventure! We're going camping at the lake! Come on, girl. Get in the car. We're ready to go."

Are you ready for your BIG adventure today? Jesus is leaving and going to His Father's house to prepare a place for us. Let's find out how we can get there. Pray and ask God to teach you.

Look at John 14:3. Touch each word as you say it out loud.

JOHN 14:3 "If I go and prepare a place for you, I will come again and receive you to Myself, that where I am, there you may be also."

Look at John 14:3. **WHAT** will Jesus do after He prepares a place for us? Trace the answer on the lines below. Say it out loud.

Jesus said, I will...

come again

and...

receive

you to

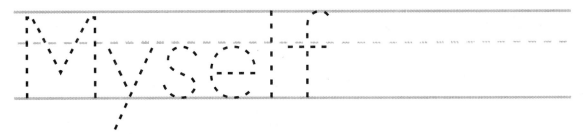

Did you know Jesus is coming back for us? **HOW** exciting is that?

Look back at John 14:3 on page 139. **WHAT** will Jesus do when He comes back? **WHERE** will He take us? Say it out loud. Circle the correct answer below.

**Jesus will take us with Him.**

**Jesus will leave us here and go back to heaven.**

Look at John 14:4 below. Touch each word as you say it out loud.

JOHN 14:4 "And you know the way where I am going."

Look back at John 14:4. **WHAT** does Jesus tell the disciples? Say it out loud.

Draw a purple oval ⬭ around the words *the way*.

Look at John 14:5 below. Touch each word as you say it out loud.

> JOHN 14:5 "Thomas said to Him, 'Lord, we do not know where You are going, how do we know the way?'"

Look back at John 14:5. **WHAT** does Thomas say to Jesus? Say it out loud.

Draw a purple oval around the words *the way*.

Jesus has just told the disciples He is going to His Father's house to prepare a place for them. And He is coming back to get them. But Thomas is confused. He tells Jesus he doesn't know the way.

**HOW** about you? Do you know **WHAT** "the way" is?

You'll find out tomorrow. Kate's head is hanging out the car window. She can't wait to get to the lake so she can find out too!

# WHAT Is the Way?

"How much longer, Dad?" Cooper asked. "Are you sure this is the right way?"

"I'm sure," Cooper's dad answered. "It's not much farther. Once we set up the tents, you and Callie can go fishing with Kate."

"All right!" Cooper and Callie high-fived each other, and Kate licked Callie's face.

Don't forget to talk to God.

Yesterday Thomas told Jesus he didn't know the way.

Look at John 14:6 to see **WHAT** Jesus tells Thomas. Touch each word as you say it out loud.

> JOHN 14:6 "Jesus said to him, 'I am the way, and the truth, and the life; no one comes to the Father but through Me.'"

Look at John 14:6. **HOW** does Jesus answer Thomas?

**WHO** is Jesus? Say it out loud.

Draw a purple cross symbol like this _____ over the words that tell us **WHO** Jesus is. Color the inside yellow.

Look back at John 14:6. **WHAT** is the only way to the Father? Trace the answer below. Say it out loud.

No one comes to the Father but through...

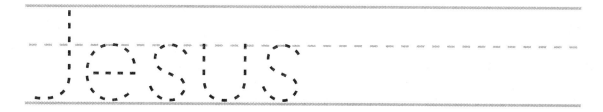

Some people believe that you can choose your own way to heaven. Is that the truth? Say it out loud.

Look at John 14:6 again. **WHAT** does Jesus say? **WHO** can choose their own way to come to the Father?

Say it out loud.

Draw a red oval ⬭ around the words *no one*.

No one can come to God their own way. Jesus tells us the ONLY way to the Father is through Him.

**WHO** is Jesus? Trace the answer on the line below. Touch each word as you say it out loud.

Jesus is...

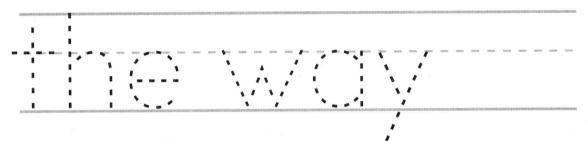

God sent Jesus to die on the cross to pay for our sins and save us. Jesus is our Savior. The ONLY way to God is through His only begotten Son, Jesus! Jesus is the way.

Look back at John 14:6 on page 143. We know Jesus is the way. **WHAT** else did Jesus tell Thomas about Himself? Trace the answer on the line below.

Jesus is...

Other people may tell you that Jesus is a good teacher but that He isn't God. They are wrong! That's not what God's Word and Jesus says. Jesus tells us He is God, and Jesus doesn't lie. **WHAT** did we just learn?

We can believe Jesus because Jesus is the TRUTH.

Look back at John 14:6 on page 143. **WHAT** is the third thing Jesus says about Himself? Trace it on the line below.

Jesus is...

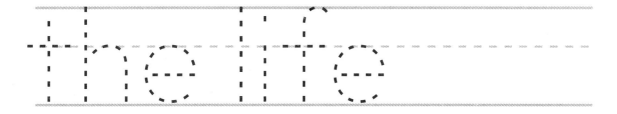

When we believe in Jesus, we receive eternal life. We are going to live forever with God because Jesus is life and Jesus lives in us when we believe.

You have discovered the only way to heaven. Salvation is through Jesus. When we believe in **WHO** Jesus is, tell Him we are sorry for our sins, and ask Him to forgive us, Jesus saves us! We become children of God.

And one day, because Jesus loves us so much, when God's time is just right, Jesus will come back and take us to live with Him!

So, **WHAT** is the only way to God? Shout it out loud!

**WHO** is Jesus? Shout it out!

All right! Now, look at the maze below to find the ONLY way to the Father.

Find the number 1 stone. Follow the path by coloring the stones in order from 1 to 10.

Now write the words from each stone you colored in order on the lines below.

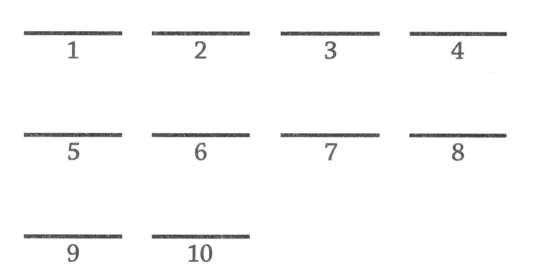

| 1 | 2 | 3 | 4 |
|---|---|---|---|

| 5 | 6 | 7 | 8 |
|---|---|---|---|

| 9 | 10 |
|---|---|

All right! The ONLY way to God is through Jesus!

You did great!

# Jesus Is Our Peace

"Come on, Callie, let's take Kate fishing," Cooper said.

"Oh, no!" Callie called out. "Kate sees a duck."

"Wait, Kate!" Cooper shouted. "Don't jump in the lake!"

Splash—it was too late! Kate is in the lake. Kate loves ducks!

"Come, Kate! Get out of the lake," Cooper yelled. "No, Kate, don't shake!" But it was too late. Kate shook water all over Callie and Cooper.

"Come, Kate. Let's dry off and sit by the campfire to see **WHAT** we can learn about Jesus. We can try fishing again tomorrow. You are one wild pup when you see a duck!"

**WHAT** will you learn about Jesus today? Have you prayed?

Look at John 16:33 on the next page. Touch each word as you say it out loud.

JOHN 16:33 "These things I have spoken to you, so that in Me you may have peace. In the world you have tribulation, but take courage; I have overcome the world."

Look at John 16:33. **WHAT** will you have in Jesus? Say it out loud. Trace the answer on the lines below.

In Jesus you have...

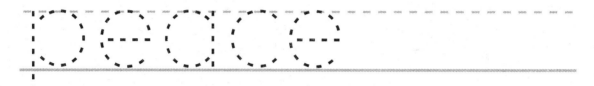

Look at John 16:33 above again. Color the word *peace* yellow.

**WHAT** will you have in the world? Say it out loud. Circle the correct answer below.

**peace**                    **tribulation**

Look back at John 16:33. Draw a black oval  around the word *tribulation*.

In the world we will have tribulation (trouble and hard times). But **WHAT** do we have in Jesus? Say it out loud.

Isn't that AWESOME? The world brings tribulation, but in Jesus we can have peace!

Look back at John 16:33 on page 150. When you have tribulation, **WHAT** are you to do?

Say it out loud. Trace the answer on the lines below.

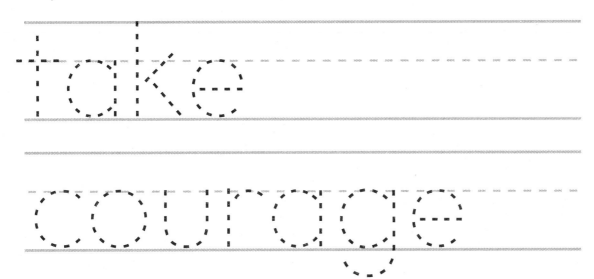

You are to be courageous—to have cheer.

**HOW** can you be courageous and full of cheer when you are going through tribulation (trouble) in this world?

Look back at John 16:33 on page 150. **WHAT** did Jesus do? Say it out loud.

Trace **WHAT** Jesus did on the lines on the next page.

Jesus has...

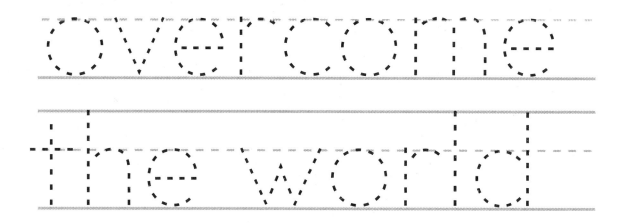

All right! When we have troubles and hard times, we can have peace in Jesus because Jesus has overcome the world! What awesome POWER! Jesus has won the victory! Jesus defeated sin and Satan, the ruler of this world, when He died on the cross to pay for our sins, was buried, and was resurrected. God raised Him from the dead on the third day! Jesus is the Overcomer!

And when you are saved by faith in Jesus and become God's child, you become an overcomer too! God tells us in 1 John 5:5 that we overcome the world by our faith in Jesus—by believing what God says about Him! How cool is that?

In this world we will have trouble, but we can take courage. **WHY**? **WHAT** did Jesus do? Fill in the blanks below.

Jesus has o ____ ____ ____ ____ ____ ____ ____ the world!

Shout it out loud!

Color the picture below to show Jesus has overcome the world.

# WHO Is Jesus?

"Sit, Kate!" Cooper gave Kate a sign. "Don't rock the boat. It's time to fish for breakfast. Wouldn't it be cool to fish with Jesus?"

"Well," Callie said, "we 'fished' with Jesus when we shared **WHO** He is with Imani, Mozzie, and Stephen."

"That's true," Cooper agreed. "We were 'fishers of kids.' Hey, Callie—I caught a fish!"

"Me too!" Callie said, reeling in her catch. "Let's go show Mom and Dad our BIG catch. Stop, Kate!" Callie pulled on her fishing rod to get her fish out of Kate's mouth. "Catch your own fish!"

Cooper laughed at Callie and Kate. "Let's hurry. We need to talk to God and eat our fish so we can review all we learned about Jesus to become 'fishers of men.'"

Talk to God and tell Him thank You for everything He has taught you about Jesus. Ask Him to show you **HOW** to follow Him and become "fishers of men."

Now you are ready for your BIG catch today!

Let's play a matching game to see if you can remember all the things you learned about Jesus in the Gospel of John.

Look at page 156. On the left side of the page are words that describe **WHO** Jesus is. On the right side are titles to match each description of Jesus.

Draw a line from the description on the left to match the title of **WHO** Jesus is on the right.

## WHO Is Jesus?

I am God's message.

Jesus is the resurrection and the life.

I shine in the darkness.

Jesus is the Word.

I have power over death.

Jesus is the Lamb of God.

I take away the sins of the world.

Jesus is the Light.

In the world you will have trouble.

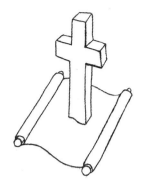

Jesus is the Christ.

All things were made through Me.

Jesus is our peace—Jesus has overcome the world.

I am the promised Messiah.

Jesus is the Son of God.

I left heaven to be born as a baby.

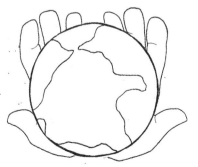

Jesus is Creator.

God sent Me to save the world.

Jesus is the way, the truth, and the life.

I lead, guide, take care of, and protect My sheep.

Jesus is Savior.

I am the ONLY way to the Father.

Jesus is King of Israel.

I will rule Israel.

Jesus is the good shepherd.

Woo-hoo! Kate is so excited about all you have learned about Jesus. She is jumping up and down, barking, and wagging her tail.

You did it! You learned to read the Bible, God's Word.

You also discovered **WHO** Jesus is.

There is one more thing to discover before our adventure ends. Look at John 20:31 below. Touch each word as you say it out loud.

> JOHN 20:31 "These have been written so that you may believe that Jesus is the Christ, the Son of God; and that believing you may have life in His name."

Look at John 20:31. John tells us **WHY** he wrote the Gospel of John. Trace the answer on the lines below.

These things were written so that you may...

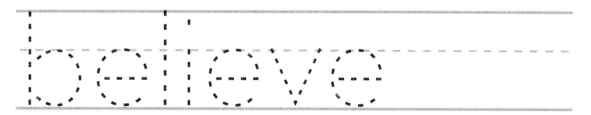

that Jesus is the...

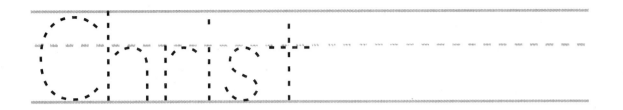

the...

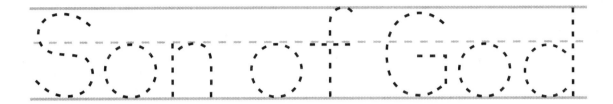

John wrote the Gospel of John so that you and I and the whole world can know **WHO** Jesus is and believe in Him.

Jesus is the Christ, the Son of God—God's promised one.

If you believe in Jesus, you will have life in His name. That's **WHY** you need to know **WHO** Jesus is.

Jesus is the ONLY way to the Father.

Salvation is a free gift from God. You can't earn it. You have to believe, to trust in **WHO** Jesus is and follow Him. Amazing! God loves you so much!

**WHAT** is your favorite thing you learned about Jesus? Draw and color a picture, sing a song, write a poem, or say a prayer about your favorite thing you learned about Jesus.

You did great! We are so proud of you!

Cooper and Callie want to give you a high-five!

Kate just wants to give you a good face-licking!

Don't forget all you have learned. Tell others **WHO** Jesus is.

And don't forget to follow Him! Do the things Jesus says to do. Be like Him.

Say thank You to God for His gift of Jesus.

Shout out **WHO** loves you!

Way to go! Cooper, Callie, and Kate can't wait to go on another adventure in God's Word with you!

# Beginner Inductive Bible Studies

This series is specially designed for children ages four to seven. Each book helps children build a familiarity with and love for God's Word at an early age. Kids will also develop reading and writing readiness as well as thinking and reasoning skills.

Children will have a blast following the many adventures of Cooper and Callie and their faithful canine companion Kate as they go on a quest for Bible knowledge. This unique series makes use of all learning styles—visual, auditory, read-write, and kinesthetic—to create a fun and memorable experience for every child.

Join Cooper, Callie, and Kate on another exciting adventure as they continue learning to read and study the Bible for themselves. In this first book of the Beginner Inductive Bible Study series, Cooper, Callie, and Kate search in Genesis 1 for clues to find out who created the world and how it happened. They also discover life-changing information about what this Creator is like and how they fit into His plan for the world.

## Also from Harvest House Publishers...
## The Best Inductive Studies for Kids Age 8 to 12

The studies in the Discover 4 Yourself® series help tweens find out for themselves what the Bible is all about—and give them exciting ways to do it! These hands-on books help teach the basic skills of Bible study and prepare tweens for a lifetime of discovering God's Word.

### Old Testament

*God's Amazing Creation*
(Genesis 1–2)

*Digging Up the Past*
(Genesis 3–11)

*Abraham, God's Brave Explorer*
(Genesis 11-25)

*Extreme Adventures with God*
(Genesis 24–36)

*Joseph, God's Superhero*
(Genesis 37–50)

*God Has Big Plans for You, Esther*
(Esther)

*You're a Brave Man, Daniel*
(Daniel 1–6)

*Fast-Forward to the Future*
(Daniel 7–12)

*Wrong Way, Jonah!*
(Jonah)

### New Testament

*Jesus in the Spotlight*
(John 1–10)

*Jesus—Awesome Power, Awesome Love*
(John 11–16)

*Jesus—to Eternity and Beyond*
(John 17–21)

*Becoming God's Champion*
(2 Timothy)

*Boy, Have I Got Problems!*
(James)

*Bible Prophecy for Kids*
(Revelation 1–7)

*A Sneak Peek into the Future*
(Revelation 8–22)

### Topical

*God, What's Your Name?*
*Lord, Teach Me to Pray for Kids*
*How to Study Your Bible for Kids*
*Cracking the Covenant Code*

To learn more about Harvest House books and to read sample chapters, visit our website:

**www.harvesthousepublishers.com**

**HARVEST HOUSE PUBLISHERS**
EUGENE, OREGON